Susta

by
Christ
Consider the Cost

*Original Poetry
from*

*Nadine Sallins*

# *Sustained and Ordained by Christ, Consider the Cost*

## *Copyright 2021 by Nadine Sallins*

# Dedication

Lord

(Jesus Christ)

I dedicate this book to you
lord, because you hold our soul

When we turned left, you made
things right, to show your in
control

# Introduction

Many times, we overlook or often don't take the time out to really consider the cost Jesus paid on calvary for our sins. We most of the time take it for granted or maybe don't have the full understanding of what it meant for Jesus and his love for us and our need for a savior. Without God we can do nothing. So, we live today because he died for us.

My poetry is based on the life Jesus suffered for us considering the cost to help save the lost. We were lost in our sins and in need of a savior and he came willingly to pay with his life for us. That we may really, truly, live for eternity with him. Our life is not our own, we were bought with a price, the price was Jesus. Let us keep our eyes on the cross, letting our lives reflect what was done for us, that we may live for him.

# ORDAINED

*Considering the Cost*

*I will do a new thing in you, just wait, and see*

*A living sacrifice, that's what I will be*

*Wounded for your transgression, bruised for your iniquities*

*The old, rugged cross, was my responsibility*

*Considering the cost, I suffered in loss*

*Spat at and beaten, my garments were tossed*

*I Came in the form of no reputation*

*To show my love, with no speculation*

*My blood is for cleansing, redemption of sins*

*With this being done, your new life begins*

*Sacrificed my Life, to offer eternal life in me*

*Without this taken place, you would not be free*

*I have no regrets, there is no shame*

*My love for you, remains the same*

*I am the love that never dies*

*Give strength to the weak, without compromise*

*When you think of me, it's eternity*

*Where my spirit resides, there is liberty*

*I am, the one who made you free*

*Gave sight to the blind, that they may see*

*In all your getting, get understanding*

*Of whom I am, and what I'm commanding*

*Man was made in the image of me*

*To change the world, and set the captive free*

*To make a difference, the important part*

*To trust in me, with all your heart*

*To stay on the path that leads to life*

*Without any arguing, bitterness, or strife*

*To come together in unity*

*Without love you cannot be, in tune with me*

*The gifts I give comes with the key*

*That will soon unlock your destiny*

*The flood gates of heaven will pour upon you*

*The gift of life will favor you too*

*So, take my word, and study it right*

*I will show you love, give understanding, and insight*

*My ways not your ways, my thoughts not your thoughts*

*Keeping your best interest at heart, making you fit for the part*

*Be still know that I am God, sit back, buckle up, enjoy the ride*

*Then you will see what you have in me, boasting inside, without any pride*

*I will never leave or forsake you, my word is always true*

*I know the plans I have for you; did I not explain this to you?*

*Fighting the good fight of faith, is what believers do*

*Putting on the whole armor of God is what gets you through*

*Ready in season and out of season is what you were told to be*

*With this in mind, you will do just fine, proclaiming victory*

*Not looking to the left or to the right but looking straight ahead*

*For the heavenly price of Jesus Christ who lives and is not dead*

*To live a life of holiness, is pleasing to our Lord*

*He gave us life in exchange for death, the price we could not afford*

*We give praises to you Lord, where praise is due*

*We are wired to worship, and we glorify you*

*Whatever we put our hands to do,
we do sincerely unto you*

*The harvest is plentiful, and the
laborers are few*

*This is how to demonstrate, our
love for you*

*No greater love, has no man than
this*

*To lay down his life, betrayed with
a kiss*

*You stuck with the plans, with the
world in your hands*

*With grace and love, sent from
above*

*We now proclaim your DNA*

*Your will be done Lord, have your
way*

# WHO I AM

I am a child of the most high God,
With wings like eagles, flying high
by your side


I am fearfully and wonderfully
made through Christ Jesus
Protected and perfected having
nothing between us

I am seated in heavenly places
with the Lord God
What I'm feeling inside, it's too
exciting to hide

In Christ Jesus I have the victory
Where I am able to see his ability

I am an overcomer just like the
Lord
The price he paid no man can
afford

I am a chosen generation, a royal
priesthood
What that meant to me at first, I
never understood

I am a peculiar person, set apart
as his kind
To do exploits in his name,
keeping the lost in mind

I can do all things, through Christ
Jesus who strengthens me
Heal the sick, raise the dead,
make the blind see

When I decree a thing, it shall be
done
His works, his power, his chosen
one

I am infused with the power of the
Holy Ghost
A child of a king, that is, not like
most

I am a soldier, in the army of the
Lord
Where it's all about order,
together, one accord

Brought with a price, Jesus
sacrificed his life
Hung on a tree, where I found my
identity

# TRUST IN HIM

*I will trust in you Lord with all my heart,*
*Wait on you Lord, and be set apart*

*When I'm frustrated, and don't understand,*
*I consult with you Lord, the one with my plan*

*So, I thank you Lord, for the abundant life,*
*What a pleasure to be called your bride/wife*

*I am wired to worship, and call on your name*
*Setting the atmosphere, without any shame*

*Continuing in your presence, communing with you*
*With fervent prayers, in honesty too*

*I will trust in you Lord, this you will see*
*Continue in my faith, you believe in me*

*By my faith mountains move, and are thrown into the sea*
*This is the supernatural, that lives inside of me*

*My body is your temple, the place*
*where you reside*
*Holy, pure, and precious, with*
*love I will abide*

*I will trust you Lord, you always*
*make a way*
*Out of no way, you speak things*
*align and obey*

*When put to the test, focus on*
*what's best*
*But not on the mess, putting*
*death to the flesh*

*My food is to finish, the work*
*before me*
*To serve, love, give, to the less*
*fortunate and needy*

*To love, honor, and obey, is the key to success*
*Just trust in the Lord, he will handle the rest*
*I will trust in him, to help me get it done*
*In the end he will say, well done my good and faithful one*

# OBEDIENCE

Obedience God said, is better
than sacrifice
Do what he tells you, treat
everyone nice

When I'm in need, I sow my seed
I am his breed, with his blood I
plead

I am his daughter, full of light
a warrior in prayer, I know how to
fight

Like David a man, after God's
own heart

Nothing in this world, can keep us
apart

When the enemy comes, and try
to attack
It is good to know, you have my
back

With two or three gathered, there
you're in the mist
Your presence is so powerful,
always willing to assist

I won't take for granted, what
Jesus Christ did for me
nothing was done on my part; it
was all love for you and me

To obey sometimes is really hard,
without knowing what's ahead

Jesus died, in three days came
alive, by doing what his father
said

Beloved father I will obey, the
calling you have on my life
Because in your word it clearly
states, obedience is better than
sacrifice

# FAITHFULNESS

*Great is your faithfulness, the
love and grace you give
In you we have our being, and
also strength to live*

*We walk by faith and not by sight,
for what we see is temporal
We walk in light like you are in
light, we invest in life eternal*

*You are not man that you should
lie, your word won't come back
void
He who promised is faithful, but
enemy comes to destroy*

*The opposite of faith is fear, and
this is not of God
Talk to the Lord in prayer
believing, and your fear will
shortly subside*

*Live with a heart of gratefulness,
this too is very wise
Appreciate all you have, with no
room to compromise*

*Faithful to our calling, is what we
ought to be
Procrastination and slothfulness,
forfeit's our destiny*

*Walk worthy of your calling, with
excitement, full of grace
With God given strength inside
you, to keep you in the race*

*Be about the father's business,*
*don't take him for granted at all*
*soles at stake we must be awake,*
*to take heed unless we fall*

# TRUTH

The meaning of truth is a
statement or fact, that is usually
rejected
When we were lost, you paid the
cost, and now we are connected

You are the truth, way, and the
life, where all men can be free
We lift our hands in total praise,
we have victory

Truth be told your love for us, we
surely don't deserve
You hate the sin but love the
sinner, our life is now preserved

Because of truth we know for
sure, our rights in where we stand
It's by your grace and not our
works, and all by your command

Sin by nature is what we are, it
came through Adam and Eve
But Jesus Christ came to give
life, for all that will believe

Thank God for truth for he is
truth, and not a man that he
should lie
We have his book the living word,
that lives and will never die

## *LOVE*

Love is kind, gentle, patient,
obedient
Forgiving, caring, self-controlled,
expedient

Our Lord is all of the above, and
so much more
He downloads in our spirit, like
never before

He is our breath and, our bread of
life
Strong tower, fortress, refuge and
insight

Love is powerful, it covers a
multitude of sins

It brings healing to the sick, and
put death to an end

When you think of love, think on
the loss
With Jesus love, considering the
cost

# THE HEART

*The heart is what, we need to*
*live,*
*Pumps blood that flows, through*
*the body that gives*
*Nutrients to the bone, and all its*
*parts*
*To stand for love, that's where it*
*starts*
*When you think of love, think of*
*our God*
*Take a moment look up, and step*
*aside*

*Connect with his son, and learn*
*to abide*
*He is always here for you, and*
*the reason he died*
*So always be pure, holy, and set*
*apart,*
*For our God knows, sees, and*
*discerns the heart*

# THE MIND

*The mind is a terrible thing to
waste
Be careful in thinking, without
moving in haste*

*Our Lord God will keep us in
perfect peace,
With our mind staying on him, the
negative will seize*

*God is perfect, loving, gentle, and
kind
With his protection and guidance,
you will surely be fine*

*Have no fear our God is here, to
serve and help so let's be clear*

*With Godly fear you will find, how*
*to prepare the heart and mind*

# THE SOUL

The living soul God's breath into
man
Given to all, across the land

Within the body, it sits inside
Within our character, it rests and
resides

The soul is God's most precious
thing,
With this in mind, our hearts can
sing

We give Praises to our Lord; this
is how we roll

trusting him with our whole heart,
mind, body and soul

# THE SPIRIT

Test the spirit by the holy spirit,
and see if it's of God
Know them by their fruit, don't be
taken for a bribe


The holy spirit is our helper, in
this we will obey
And when the evil spirit comes,
with prayer it goes away


Do not be drunk off of wine, or
pretend you did not hear it
Be not enticed by what feels nice,
they call it wine and spirits

Stay in the spirit, as God is in
spirit, and you won't fulfill the
flesh
Obey the boss or pay the cost,
like a dog turning back to his
mess

# THE BODY

*The body is the temple of the holy*
*spirit, so watch what goes in*
*It's holy, pure, sacred, and real,*
*repent and turn from sin*


*Made up of many parts and also*
*connected as a whole*
*With God as the head, and we as*
*the parts, attached to the soul*


*We Treasure the body, all*
*together so we will abide*
*Serving each other hand and*
*hand, working side by side*

# LIFE

Life is what we make it, and
dreams we have someday
Leaning on the Lord, for him to
have his way

Real Life is through Jesus Christ,
to trust and obey
Look to him for everything, he
has the final say

He also is our life support, without
him we will die
Lift your hands in total praise, to
him that hear your cry

# DEATH

Death is something Jesus paid
for, the penalty of our sins
On the cross he paid the cost, it
is finished and put to an end

Death to the flesh is what is best,
to really, truly live
My heart and soul is what I'm
told, I must prepare to give

Denying yourself we must do
daily, along with carrying our
cross
With hands to the plow and not
turning back, also considering the
cost

# Acknowledgement

### *My thank you poem to the lord*

I considered the cost you paid for me,
Enduring the hurt, pain, in suffering

Remembering the time, keeping it in my mind
In no man you will find, what you did was so
kind

Not looking at the neglect or disrespect
Just showing love, you came to protect

I wanna thank you lord, for loving me
For not walking away, and helping me see

What you endured was willingly, what man
would have tossed
You paid the cost, that all may live, and none
be lost

So thank you lord, with my deepest sincerity
Considering the cost, we live for eternity

# About the Author

A mother of three and a grandmother of five Nadine is looking forward to her next book hoping to touch, encourage, and inspire people all over the world that are struggling with mental, physical, and emotional abuse.

Professionally Nadine Sallins has 21 years' experience in the nursing field and has a passion for helping others. She has dedicated her life to giving and helping those that are less fortunate. Nadine was born 1970 in the state of Pennsylvania and is currently a resident in the borough of Sharon Hill.

*Thank you for reading my book!*

*I really appreciate all of your feedback, and I love hearing what you have to say.*

*Your input will help make the next version of this book and my future books better and better.*

*Please leave me an honest helpful review on Amazon letting me know what you thought of the book.*

*May God bless you!*

*Nadine Sallins*

Made in the USA
Columbia, SC
24 February 2024

32059904R00029